Chorizo Hash

Makes 4 servings

2 **russet potatoes, cut into ½-inch pieces**

3 **teaspoons salt, divided**

8 **ounces Mexican chorizo sausage**

1 **yellow onion, chopped**

½ **red bell pepper, chopped (about ½ cup)**

Fried, poached or scrambled eggs (optional)

Avocado slices (optional)

Fresh cilantro leaves (optional)

1. Preheat grill grid over campfire.

2. Fill medium saucepan half full with water. Add potatoes and 2 teaspoons salt; bring to a boil. Cook 8 minutes. (Potatoes will be firm.) Drain.

3. Meanwhile, remove and discard casing from chorizo. Crumble chorizo into large cast iron skillet; cook and stir over medium coals 5 minutes or until lightly browned. Add onion and bell pepper; cook and stir 4 minutes or until vegetables are softened.

4. Stir in potatoes and remaining 1 teaspoon salt; cook 8 to 10 minutes or until vegetables are tender and potatoes are lightly browned, stirring occasionally. Serve with eggs, if desired; garnish with avocado and cilantro.

Twisted Cinnamon Sticks

Makes 8 servings

1 **cup sugar**

3 **tablespoons ground cinnamon**

1 **can (8 ounces) refrigerated crescent roll dough**

½ **cup (1 stick) butter, melted**

1. Combine sugar and cinnamon in small bowl; stir to blend. Set aside. Roll each section of dough into long strip; twist around long roasting skewers or clean sticks. Place over medium coals of campfire. Cook and turn 6 minutes or until lightly browned.

2. Remove sticks to heatproof surface. Cool slightly; remove to large serving plate. Brush with melted butter and sprinkle with cinnamon-sugar mixture.

Sausage and Cheddar Corn Bread

Makes 10 servings

1 **tablespoon vegetable oil**

½ **pound bulk pork sausage**

1 **medium onion, diced**

1 **jalapeño pepper, diced**

1 **package (about 8 ounces) corn muffin mix**

1 **cup (4 ounces) shredded Cheddar cheese, divided**

⅓ **cup milk**

1 **egg**

1. Preheat grill grid over campfire.

2. Heat oil in large cast iron skillet over medium coals. Brown sausage 6 to 8 minutes, stirring to break up meat. Add onion and jalapeño pepper; cook and stir 5 minutes or until vegetables are softened. Remove sausage mixture to medium bowl.

3. Combine corn muffin mix, ½ cup cheese, milk and egg in separate medium bowl. Pour batter into skillet. Spread sausage mixture over top. Sprinkle with remaining ½ cup cheese. Cover; cook over medium coals 15 to 20 minutes or until edges are lightly browned. Cut into wedges to serve.

Twisted
Cinnamon
Sticks

Ham and Egg Breakfast Panini

Makes 2 sandwiches

¼ **cup chopped red or green bell pepper**

2 **tablespoons sliced green onion**

1 **slice (1 ounce) smoked deli ham, chopped**

2 **eggs**

Black pepper

4 **tablespoons (½ stick) butter**

4 **slices multigrain or whole grain bread**

2 **slices (¾ ounce each) Cheddar or Swiss cheese**

1. Preheat grill grid over campfire.

2. Spray small cast iron skillet with nonstick cooking spray; heat over medium coals. Add bell pepper and green onion; cook and stir 4 minutes or until crisp-tender. Stir in ham.

3. Whisk eggs and black pepper in small bowl until well blended. Pour egg mixture into skillet; cook 2 minutes or until egg mixture is almost set, stirring occasionally.

4. Layer 1 tablespoon butter, 1 bread slice, 1 cheese slice and half of egg mixture. Top with 1 bread slice and 1 tablespoon butter.

5. Hold pie iron level over medium coals of campfire 6 minutes or until golden brown on each side, turning once. Remove to heatproof surface, carefully remove sandwich to serving plate. Repeat with remaining ingredients. Serve immediately.

Cinnamon Pecan Rolls

Makes about 18 rolls

- **4 tablespoons (½ stick) butter, melted, divided**
- **1 loaf (16 ounces) frozen bread dough, thawed according to package directions**
- **½ cup packed dark brown sugar**
- **2 teaspoons ground cinnamon**
- **½ cup chopped pecans**

1. Preheat grill grid over campfire. Brush large cast iron skillet with ½ tablespoon melted butter. Roll out dough into 18×8-inch rectangle on lightly floured surface.

2. Combine brown sugar, 3 tablespoons butter and cinnamon in medium bowl; mix well. Brush mixture evenly over dough; sprinkle with pecans. Starting with long side, roll up dough jelly-roll style; pinch seam to seal.

3. Cut crosswise into 1-inch slices; arrange slices cut sides up in prepared skillet. Cover loosely and let rise in warm place about 30 minutes or until doubled in size.

4. Brush tops of rolls with remaining ½ tablespoon butter. Cook over medium coals 10 minutes or until puffed and golden brown. Serve warm.

Caramelized Bacon

Makes 6 servings

- **12 slices (about 12 ounces) applewood-smoked bacon**
- **½ cup packed brown sugar**
- **2 tablespoons water**
- **¼ to ½ teaspoon ground red pepper**

1. Preheat grill grid over campfire. Line large rimmed baking sheet with foil. Spray wire rack with nonstick cooking spray; place on prepared baking sheet.

2. Arrange bacon in single layer on prepared wire rack. Combine brown sugar, water and ground red pepper in small bowl; mix well. Brush generously over bacon.

3. Cook 10 to 15 minutes over medium coals or until bacon is well browned. Immediately remove to serving platter; cool completely.

Cinnamon Pecan Rolls

Mediterranean Chicken Kabobs,
page 44

Patio Poultry

All-American Barbecue Grilled Chicken

Makes 4 servings

1 sheet REYNOLDS WRAP® Non-Stick Foil

6 chicken pieces

1 cup southwestern barbecue sauce

HEAT grill to medium-high. Make drainage holes in sheet of REYNOLDS WRAP® Non-Stick Foil with a large fork. Place foil sheet on grill grate with non-stick (dull) side facing up; immediately place chicken on foil.

GRILL covered 10 minutes. Turn chicken; brush chicken with barbecue sauce. Grill 10 minutes longer; turn chicken. Brush again with barbecue sauce; continue grilling until chicken is tender and reaches 180°F. Discard any remaining sauce.

Southwestern Barbecue Sauce

Add 2 teaspoons chili powder, 1 teaspoon dry mustard, ¼ teaspoon garlic powder and ¼ teaspoon cayenne pepper to barbecue sauce. Grill as directed above.

Barbecued Chicken Pizza

Makes 8 servings

3 to 4 ounces boneless, skinless chicken breasts

6 tablespoons barbecue sauce, divided

1 cup pizza sauce

1 (12-inch) pizza crust

1 can (8 oz.) DOLE® Pineapple Tidbits, drained

⅓ cup roasted red pepper strips, drained

1½ cups shredded mozzarella cheese

2 tablespoons chopped fresh parsley

- **Pound** chicken until flat. Arrange chicken on broiler pan or grill. Brush chicken with 1 tablespoon barbecue sauce. Broil 3 minutes; turn chicken and brush with 1 tablespoon barbecue sauce. Broil 3 minutes more or until chicken is no longer pink in center. Cut chicken into strips.

- **Spoon** pizza sauce over crust. Top with chicken strips, pineapple tidbits and red pepper. Drizzle remaining 4 tablespoons barbecue sauce over pizza; sprinkle with cheese and parsley.

- **Bake** at 425°F. 20 minutes or until crust is golden brown.

Garlic & Lemon Herb Marinated Chicken

Makes 4 servings

- **3 to 4 pounds bone-in chicken pieces, skinned if desired**
- **⅓ cup FRENCH'S® Honey Dijon Mustard**
- **⅓ cup lemon juice**
- **⅓ cup olive oil**
- **3 cloves garlic, minced**
- **1 tablespoon grated lemon zest**
- **1 tablespoon minced fresh thyme or rosemary**
- **1 teaspoon coarse salt**
- **½ teaspoon coarse black pepper**

1. Place chicken into resealable plastic food storage bag. Combine remaining ingredients. Pour over chicken. Marinate in refrigerator 1 to 3 hours.

2. Remove chicken from marinade. Grill chicken over medium direct heat for 35 to 45 minutes until juices run clear near bone (170°F for breast meat; 180°F for dark meat). Serve with additional mustard on the side.

Tip

This marinade is also great on whole chicken or pork chops.

Chutney Turkey Burgers

Makes 4 servings

- **1 pound ground turkey**
- **½ cup prepared chutney, divided**
- **½ teaspoon salt**
- **½ teaspoon pepper**
- **⅛ teaspoon hot pepper sauce**
- **½ cup nonfat plain yogurt**
- **1 teaspoon curry powder**
- **4 hamburger buns, split**

1. Preheat grill for direct-heat cooking.

2. In medium bowl, combine turkey, ¼ cup chutney, salt, pepper and hot pepper sauce. Shape turkey mixture into 4 burgers, approximately 3½ inches in diameter. Grill turkey burgers 5 to 6 minutes per side until 165°F is reached on meat thermometer and turkey is no longer pink in center.

3. In small bowl, combine yogurt, curry powder and remaining ¼ cup chutney.

4. To serve, place burgers on bottom halves of buns; spoon yogurt mixture over burgers and cover with top halves of buns.

National Turkey Federation

Thai Coffee Chicken Skewers

Makes 8 skewers

1¼ **pounds chicken tenders, cut crosswise into ½-inch-wide strips**

⅓ **cup soy sauce**

¼ **cup strong brewed coffee**

2 **tablespoons plus 2 teaspoons fresh lime juice, divided**

4 **cloves garlic, minced, divided**

1 **tablespoon plus 1 teaspoon grated fresh ginger, divided**

½ **teaspoon sriracha or hot chili sauce, divided**

8 **(12-inch) bamboo skewers**

½ **cup water**

¼ **cup hoisin sauce**

2 **tablespoons creamy peanut butter**

1 **tablespoon tomato paste**

1 **teaspoon sugar**

4 **green onions, cut into 1-inch pieces**

1. Combine chicken, soy sauce, coffee, 2 tablespoons lime juice, 2 cloves garlic, 1 teaspoon ginger and ¼ teaspoon sriracha in large resealable food storage bag. Seal bag; shake well to coat. Marinate chicken in refrigerator 1 to 2 hours.

2. Soak skewers in water 20 minutes. Prepare grill for direct cooking or preheat grill grid over campfire. Whisk water, hoisin sauce, peanut butter, tomato paste, sugar, remaining 1 tablespoon ginger, 2 cloves garlic, 2 teaspoons lime juice and ¼ teaspoon sriracha sauce in medium bowl until well blended; set aside.

3. Remove chicken from marinade; discard marinade. Alternately thread chicken and green onions onto skewers.

4. Grill skewers over medium heat 6 to 8 minutes or until chicken is cooked through (165°F), turning halfway through grilling time. Serve with peanut sauce.

Mesquite-Grilled Turkey

Makes 8 to 10 servings

2 cups mesquite chips, divided

1 fresh or thawed frozen turkey (10 to 12 pounds)

1 onion, peeled and quartered

1 lemon, quartered

6 fresh tarragon sprigs, divided

2 tablespoons butter, softened

Salt and black pepper

¼ cup (½ stick) butter, melted

2 tablespoons lemon juice

2 tablespoons chopped fresh tarragon *or* 2 teaspoons dried tarragon

2 cloves garlic, minced

1. Soak mesquite chips in cold water 20 minutes. Prepare grill for indirect cooking or preheat grill grid over campfire. Rinse turkey; pat dry with paper towels. Place onion, lemon and 3 tarragon sprigs in cavity. Pull skin over neck; secure with 6-inch-long metal skewer. Tuck wing tips under back; tie legs together with wet kitchen string.

2. Spread softened butter over turkey skin; sprinkle with salt and pepper. Insert meat thermometer into center of thickest part of thigh, not touching bone.

3. Drain mesquite chips; sprinkle 1 cup over coals. Place turkey, breast side up, on grid directly over drip pan. Grill turkey, covered, over medium heat 11 to 14 minutes per pound, adding 4 to 9 coals to both sides of fire each hour to maintain medium coals and adding remaining 1 cup mesquite chips after 1 hour of grilling. Meanwhile, soak remaining 3 fresh tarragon sprigs in water.

4. Combine melted butter, lemon juice, chopped tarragon and garlic in small bowl; stir to blend. Brush half of mixture over turkey during last 30 minutes of grilling. Place soaked tarragon sprigs directly on coals. Continue to grill, covered, 20 minutes. Brush with remaining butter mixture. Continue to grill, covered, about 10 minutes or until turkey is cooked through (165°F).

5. Remove turkey to large cutting board; cover loosely with foil. Let stand 15 minutes before carving. Discard onion, lemon and tarragon sprigs from cavity.

Grilled Chicken with Southern Barbecue Sauce

Makes 6 servings

½ **cup chopped onion (about 1 small)**

4 **cloves garlic, minced**

1 **can (16 ounces) tomato sauce**

¾ **cup water**

3 **tablespoons packed light brown sugar**

3 **tablespoons chili sauce**

2 **teaspoons chili powder**

2 **teaspoons dried thyme**

2 **teaspoons Worcestershire sauce**

¾ **teaspoon ground red pepper**

½ **teaspoon ground cinnamon**

½ **teaspoon black pepper**

6 **boneless skinless chicken breasts (2¼ pounds)**

1. Spray medium skillet with nonstick cooking spray; heat over medium heat. Add onion and garlic; cook and stir 5 minutes or until tender.

2. Stir in tomato sauce, water, brown sugar, chili sauce, chili powder, thyme, Worcestershire sauce, red pepper, cinnamon and black pepper; bring to a boil. Reduce heat to low and simmer, uncovered, 30 minutes or until mixture is reduced to about 1½ cups. Reserve ¾ cup sauce for basting. Meanwhile, prepare grill for indirect cooking or preheat grill grid over campfire.

3. Grill chicken, covered, over medium heat 40 to 45 minutes or until cooked through (165°F), turning chicken several times and basting occasionally with reserved sauce.

4. Heat remaining sauce in same skillet over medium heat; spoon over chicken.

Greek Chicken Burgers with Cucumber Yogurt Sauce

Makes 4 servings

½ **cup plus 2 tablespoons plain nonfat Greek yogurt**

½ **medium cucumber, peeled, seeded and finely chopped**

Juice of ½ lemon

3 **cloves garlic, minced, divided**

2 **teaspoons finely chopped fresh mint *or* ½ teaspoon dried mint**

⅛ **teaspoon salt**

⅛ **teaspoon ground white pepper**

1 **pound ground chicken**

¾ **cup (3 ounces) crumbled feta cheese**

4 **large kalamata olives, rinsed, patted dry and minced**

1 **egg**

½ **to 1 teaspoon dried oregano**

¼ **teaspoon black pepper**

Mixed baby lettuce (optional)

Fresh mint leaves (optional)

1. Combine yogurt, cucumber, lemon juice, 2 cloves garlic, 2 teaspoons chopped mint, salt and white pepper in medium bowl; mix well. Cover and refrigerate until ready to serve.

2. Prepare grill for direct cooking or preheat grill grid over campfire. Combine chicken, cheese, olives, egg, oregano, black pepper and remaining 1 clove garlic in large bowl; mix well. Shape mixture into four patties.

3. Spray grill pan with nonstick cooking spray; heat over medium-high heat. Grill patties 5 to 7 minutes per side or until cooked through (165°F).

4. Serve burgers with sauce and mixed greens, if desired. Garnish with mint leaves.

Grilled Vietnamese-Style Chicken Wings

Makes 6 to 8 servings

3 **pounds chicken wings**

⅓ **cup honey**

¼ to ½ cup sliced lemongrass

¼ **cup fish sauce**

2 **tablespoons chopped garlic**

2 **tablespoons chopped shallots**

2 **tablespoons chopped fresh ginger**

2 **tablespoons lime juice**

2 **tablespoons canola oil**

Chopped fresh cilantro (optional)

1. Remove and discard wing tips. Cut each wing in half at joint. Place wings in large resealable food storage bag.

2. Combine honey, lemongrass, fish sauce, garlic, shallots, ginger, lime juice and oil in food processor; process until smooth. Pour over wings. Seal bag; turn to coat. Marinate in refrigerator 4 hours or overnight.

3. Prepare grill for direct cooking or preheat grill grid over campfire.

4. Remove wings from marinade; reserve marinade. Grill wings over medium heat 10 minutes or until browned, turning and basting occasionally with marinade. Discard any remaining marinade. Sprinkle with cilantro, if desired.

Mediterranean Chicken Kabobs

Makes 8 servings

- **2 pounds boneless skinless chicken breasts or chicken tenders, cut into 1-inch pieces**
- **1 small eggplant, peeled and cut into 1-inch pieces**
- **1 medium zucchini, cut crosswise into ½-inch slices**
- **2 medium onions, each cut into 8 wedges**
- **16 medium mushrooms, stemmed**
- **16 cherry tomatoes**
- **1 cup chicken broth**
- **⅔ cup balsamic vinegar**
- **3 tablespoons olive oil**
- **2 tablespoons dried mint**
- **4 teaspoons dried basil**
- **1 tablespoon dried oregano**

1. Alternately thread chicken, eggplant, zucchini, onions, mushrooms and tomatoes onto 16 metal skewers; place in large glass baking dish.

2. Combine broth, vinegar, oil, mint, basil and oregano in small bowl; pour over kabobs. Cover and marinate in refrigerator 2 hours, turning kabobs occasionally. Remove kabobs from marinade; discard marinade.

3. Prepare grill for direct cooking or preheat grill grid over campfire. Grill kabobs 10 to 15 minutes or until chicken is cooked through (165°F), turning kabobs halfway through cooking time.

Note

Serve over couscous, if desired.

Buffalo Chicken Drumsticks

Makes 4 servings

- 8 large chicken drumsticks (about 2 pounds)
- 3 tablespoons hot pepper sauce
- 1 tablespoon vegetable oil
- 1 clove garlic, minced
- ¼ cup mayonnaise
- 3 tablespoons sour cream
- 1 tablespoon white wine vinegar
- ¼ teaspoon sugar
- ⅓ cup (about 1½ ounces) crumbled Roquefort or blue cheese
- 2 cups hickory chips
  Celery and carrot sticks

1. Place chicken in large resealable food storage bag. Combine hot pepper sauce, oil and garlic in small bowl; pour over chicken. Seal bag; turn to coat. Marinate in refrigerator at least 1 hour or up to 24 hours for spicier flavor, turning occasionally.

2. For blue cheese dressing, combine mayonnaise, sour cream, vinegar and sugar in another small bowl. Stir in cheese; cover and refrigerate until serving.

3. Prepare grill for direct cooking or preheat grill grid over campfire. Meanwhile, soak hickory chips in cold water 20 minutes. Drain chicken, discarding marinade. Drain hickory chips; sprinkle over coals.

4. Grill chicken, covered, over medium-high heat 25 to 30 minutes or until cooked through (165°F), turning occasionally. Serve with blue cheese dressing, celery and carrot sticks.

Cajun BBQ Beer Can Chicken

Makes 12 servings

4 (12-ounce) cans beer or non-alcoholic malt beverage

1½ cups *Cattlemen's*® Award Winning Classic Barbecue Sauce

¾ cup Cajun spice or Southwest seasoning blend

3 whole chickens (3 to 4 pounds each)

12 sprigs fresh thyme

Cajun BBQ Sauce

1 cup *Cattlemen's*® Award Winning Classic Barbecue Sauce

½ cup beer or non-alcoholic malt beverage

¼ cup butter

1 tablespoon Cajun spice or Southwest seasoning blend

1. Combine *1 can* beer, *1½ cups* barbecue sauce and *½ cup* spice blend. Following manufacturer's instructions, fill marinade injection needle with marinade. Inject chickens in several places at least 1-inch deep. Place chickens into resealable plastic food storage bags. Pour any remaining marinade over chickens. Seal bag; marinate in refrigerator 1 to 3 hours or overnight.

2. Meanwhile, prepare Cajun BBQ Sauce: In saucepan, combine *1 cup* barbecue sauce, *½ cup* beer, butter and *1 tablespoon* spice blend. Simmer 5 minutes. Refrigerate and warm just before serving.

3. Open remaining cans of beer. Spill out about *½ cup* beer from each can. Using can opener, punch several holes in tops of cans. Spoon about *1 tablespoon* additional spice blend and *4 sprigs* thyme into each can. Place 1 can upright into each cavity of chicken, arranging legs forward so chicken stands upright.

4. Place chickens upright over indirect heat on barbecue grill. Cook on a covered grill on medium-high (350°F), about 1½ hours until thigh meat registers 180°F internal temperature. (Cover chickens with foil if they become too brown while cooking.) Let stand 10 minutes before serving. Using tongs, carefully remove cans from chicken. Cut into quarters to serve. Serve with Cajun BBQ Sauce.

Pineapple Chicken Kabobs

Makes 8 servings

2 pounds boneless skinless chicken breasts, cut into 1-inch pieces

2 large bell peppers (any color), cut into 1-inch pieces

1 (20-ounce) can pineapple chunks (juice reserved)

1 medium red onion, cut into 1-inch pieces

¼ teaspoon garlic powder

Salt and black pepper

1. Soak eight wooden skewers in water 20 minutes.

2. Alternately thread chicken, bell peppers, pineapple and onion onto skewers; place in large glass baking dish. Combine reserved pineapple juice, garlic powder, salt and black pepper in small bowl; pour over kabobs. Cover; marinate in refrigerator 2 hours, turning kabobs occasionally.

3. Prepare grill for direct cooking or preheat grill grid over campfire. Remove kabobs from marinade; discard marinade.

4. Grill kabobs 10 to 15 minutes or until chicken is cooked through (165°F), turning kabobs halfway through cooking time.

Ginger-Lime Chicken Thighs

Makes 2 to 4 servings

⅓ cup vegetable oil

3 tablespoons lime juice

3 tablespoons honey

2 teaspoons grated fresh ginger *or* 1 teaspoon ground ginger

¼ to ½ teaspoon red pepper flakes

6 boneless skinless chicken thighs

1. Combine oil, lime juice, honey, ginger and red pepper flakes in small bowl. Place chicken in large resealable food storage bag. Add ½ cup marinade; reserve remaining marinade. Seal bag; turn to coat. Marinate in refrigerator 30 to 60 minutes, turning occasionally.

2. Prepare grill for direct cooking or preheat grill grid over campfire.

3. Remove chicken from marinade; discard marinade. Grill chicken over medium-high heat 12 minutes or until chicken is cooked through (165°F), turning once. Brush with reserved marinade during last 5 minutes of cooking.

Pineapple
Chicken Kabobs

Honey and Mustard Glazed Chicken

Makes 4 to 5 servings

1 **whole chicken (4 to 5 pounds)**

1 **tablespoon vegetable oil**

¼ **cup honey**

2 **tablespoons Dijon mustard**

1 **tablespoon soy sauce**

½ **teaspoon salt**

½ **teaspoon ground ginger**

¼ **teaspoon black pepper**

1. Prepare grill for indirect cooking or preheat grill grid over campfire.

2. Remove giblets from chicken cavity and discard. Pull chicken skin over neck; secure with metal skewer. Tuck wings under back; tie legs together with wet string. Lightly brush chicken with oil.

3. Combine honey, mustard, soy sauce, salt, ginger and pepper in small bowl; set aside.

4. Place chicken, breast side up, on grid directly over drip pan. Grill, covered, over medium-high heat 1 hour 30 minutes or until cooked through (165°F) for both light and dark meat. Brush with glaze every 10 minutes during last 30 minutes of cooking time.*

5. Remove chicken to large cutting board; tent with foil. Let stand 15 minutes before carving. Internal temperature will continue to rise 5°F to 10°F during stand time.

If using grill with heat on one side (rather than around drip pan), rotate chicken 180 degrees after 45 minutes of cooking time.

Nancy's Grilled Turkey Meatballs

Makes 5 servings

1 pound lean ground turkey breast

½ cup oatmeal

¼ cup fresh whole wheat bread crumbs

1 egg white

3 tablespoons Parmesan cheese

2 tablespoons FRENCH'S® Honey Dijon Mustard

¼ teaspoon crushed garlic

¼ teaspoon ground black pepper

1 cup pineapple chunks or wedges

1 small red bell pepper, cut into squares

1. Combine turkey, oatmeal, bread crumbs, egg white, cheese, mustard, garlic and black pepper in large bowl. Mix well and form into 25 meatballs.

2. Place 5 meatballs on each skewer, alternating with pineapple and bell pepper.

3. Cook meatballs 10 minutes on well-greased grill over medium heat until no longer pink inside, turning often. Serve with additional **FRENCH'S®** Honey Dijon Mustard on the side for dipping.

Tip

Combine ⅓ cup each **FRENCH'S®** Honey Dijon Mustard, honey and **FRANK'S® RedHot®** Cayenne Pepper Sauce. Use for dipping grilled wings, ribs and chicken.

Backyard Barbecue Burgers,
page 84

Backyard Beef

Beer-Marinated Steak

Makes 3 to 4 servings

1 **cup beer***

1 **onion, finely chopped**

½ **cup soy sauce**

¼ **teaspoon black pepper**

1½ **pounds boneless beef top sirloin steak (¾ inch thick)**

¼ **cup (1 ounce) shredded Cheddar cheese (optional)**

*Do not use reduced-calorie light beer.

1. Combine beer, onion, soy sauce and pepper in medium bowl. Place steak in large resealable food storage bag; add beer mixture. Seal bag; turn to coat steak. Refrigerate at least 8 hours or overnight, turning occasionally.

2. Prepare grill for direct cooking or preheat grill grid over campfire.

3. Drain steak, discarding marinade. Grill, covered, over medium-high heat 4 to 5 minutes per side for medium rare (145°F) or to desired doneness. If desired, sprinkle steak evenly with cheese just before removing from grill. Cut into thin slices across the grain.

Serving Suggestion

Serve with sautéed vegetables and cilantro-lime rice. For vegetables, thinly slice one of each red onion, red bell pepper and green bell pepper. Heat 1 tablespoon oil in large skillet over high heat. Add vegetables; cook and stir 5 minutes or until softened and browned. For rice, stir ¼ cup chopped fresh cilantro and 2 tablespoons lime juice into 3 cups of hot cooked rice. Season to taste with salt.

Beef and Pineapple Kabobs

Makes 4 servings

1 **boneless beef top sirloin or top round steak (about 1 pound)**

1 **small onion, finely chopped**

½ **cup teriyaki sauce**

16 **pieces (1-inch cubes) fresh pineapple**

1 **can (8 ounces) water chestnuts, drained**

1. Prepare grill for direct cooking or preheat grill grid over campfire. Cut steak into 1-inch pieces. For marinade, combine onion and teriyaki sauce in small bowl. Add beef to marinade, stirring to coat.

2. Alternately thread beef, pineapple cubes and water chestnuts onto four bamboo or thin metal skewers. (If using bamboo skewers, soak in water 20 minutes before using to prevent them from burning.)

3. Grill over medium heat 4 minutes, turning once, or until meat is cooked through. Serve immediately.

Note

Recipe can also be prepared with flank steak.

Serving Suggestion

Serve with hot cooked rice and stir-fried broccoli, mushrooms and red bell peppers.

Grilled Strip Steaks with Fresh Chimichurri

Makes 4 servings

4 **bone-in strip steaks (8 ounces each), about 1 inch thick**

¾ **teaspoon salt**

¾ **teaspoon ground cumin**

¼ **teaspoon black pepper**

Chimichurri (recipe follows)

1. Prepare grill for direct cooking or preheat grill grid over campfire. Oil grid. Sprinkle both sides of steaks with salt, cumin and pepper.

2. Grill steaks, covered, over medium-high heat 8 to 10 minutes for medium rare (145°F) or to desired doneness, turning once. Prepare and serve with Chimichurri.

Chimichurri

Makes about 1 cup

½ **cup packed fresh basil**

⅓ **cup extra virgin olive oil**

¼ **cup packed fresh parsley**

2 **tablespoons packed fresh cilantro**

2 **tablespoons fresh lemon juice**

1 **clove garlic**

½ **teaspoon salt**

½ **teaspoon grated orange peel**

¼ **teaspoon ground coriander**

⅛ **teaspoon black pepper**

Place basil, oil, parsley, cilantro, lemon juice, garlic, salt, orange peel, coriander and pepper in food processor or blender; purée.

Pizza Burger Sliders

Makes 16 servings

- **2 pounds lean ground beef**
- **1 envelope LIPTON® RECIPE SECRETS® Onion Soup Mix**
- **½ cup water**
- **16 small slices OR 2 cups shredded mozzarella cheese (about 8 ounces)**
- **16 slider-size whole wheat or regular hamburger buns**
- **2 cups RAGÚ® OLD WORLD STYLE® Pasta Sauce, heated**

1. Combine ground beef, LIPTON® RECIPE SECRETS® Onion Soup Mix and water in large bowl; shape into 16 patties.

2. Grill or broil until done. Top with cheese, then grill or broil until cheese is melted. Arrange on buns, then top with RAGÚ® OLD WORLD STYLE® Pasta Sauce.

Variation

For regular burgers, simply shape into 8 patties and use 8 slices cheese and 8 buns.

Tip

These mini burgers are sure to be a hit at your next barbecue. Shape them, then refrigerate until ready to grill.

Jerk-Spiced Beef Sirloin

Makes 12 servings

2 cups Swanson® Beef Stock

¼ cup olive oil

3 tablespoons Jamaican jerk seasoning

2 tablespoons balsamic vinegar

3 cloves garlic, minced

1 boneless beef top loin or beef sirloin steak, 2 inches thick (about 3 pounds)

1 tablespoon lemon juice

1 tablespoon chopped fresh cilantro leaves

1. Stir the stock, oil, seasoning, vinegar and garlic in a shallow, nonmetallic dish or gallon size resealable plastic bag. Add the steak and turn to coat. Cover the dish or seal the bag and refrigerate for 8 hours, turning the steak over a few times during marinating.

2. Lightly oil the grill rack and heat the grill to medium. Remove the steak from the marinade and pour the marinade in a 1-quart saucepan.

3. Heat the marinade over medium-high heat to a boil. Reduce the heat to low. Cook for 10 minutes. Stir in the lemon juice and cilantro. Keep warm.

4. Grill the steak for 28 minutes for medium-rare or to desired doneness, turning once during grilling. Slice the steak and serve with the lemon-cilantro sauce.

Kitchen Tip

Marinate the steak and refrigerate for up to 24 hours. When ready to serve, prepare as directed above.

Asian Marinated Flank Steak

Makes 4 servings

1 pound beef flank steak

¼ cup soy sauce

2 tablespoons rice vinegar or white wine vinegar

1 tablespoon chili garlic sauce or 1 teaspoon hot chili oil

2 teaspoons dark sesame oil

2 tablespoons chopped fresh cilantro (optional)

1. Place steak in large resealable food storage bag. Combine soy sauce, vinegar, chili garlic sauce and sesame oil in small bowl; pour over steak in bag. Close bag securely. Turn to coat steak on all sides. Refrigerate at least 2 hours or up to 48 hours.

2. Prepare grill for direct cooking or preheat grill grid over campfire. Remove steak from bag; discard marinade. Grill steak, covered, over medium-hot coals 3 to 4 inches from heat source, 4 to 5 minutes per side to medium doneness (160°F). (Do not overcook, or steak will be tough.) Remove steak to large cutting board. Tent with foil; let stand 5 minutes. Carve steak crosswise across grain into thin slices; garnish with cilantro.

Serving Suggestion

Serve with quick-cooking brown rice and a salad of thinly sliced cucumber and white onion splashed with rice vinegar and a pinch of sugar.

Beer Grilled Steaks

Makes 4 servings

1 cup light-colored beer, such as lager

¼ cup soy sauce

2 tablespoons molasses

2 cloves garlic, minced

½ teaspoon salt

¼ teaspoon black pepper

4 beef rib eye steaks, 1 inch thick (4 to 6 ounces each)

1. Whisk beer, soy sauce, molasses, garlic, salt and pepper in small bowl. Place steaks in large resealable food storage bag; add beer mixture. Marinate in refrigerator at least 2 hours.

2. Prepare grill for direct cooking or preheat grill grid over campfire. Grill steaks, covered, over high heat 8 to 10 minutes per side to at least 145°F or desired degree of doneness.

Greek-Style Steak Sandwiches

Makes 8 sandwiches

2 teaspoons dried oregano

1 beef flank steak (about 1½ pounds)

4 pita bread rounds, sliced in half crosswise

1 small cucumber, thinly sliced

1 tomato, cut into thin wedges

½ cup sliced red onion

½ cup crumbled feta cheese

¼ cup red wine vinaigrette

1 cup plain yogurt

1. Rub oregano over both sides of steak. Place on plate; cover and refrigerate 30 to 60 minutes.

2. Prepare grill for direct cooking or preheat grill grid over campfire. Grill steak, covered, over medium-high heat 17 to 21 minutes or to desired doneness, turning once. Remove steak to large cutting board. Tent with foil; let stand 10 minutes before slicing.

3. Meanwhile, grill pita halves 1 minute per side or until warm. Slice steak against the grain into thin strips; divide meat among pita halves. Top with cucumber, tomato, onion and cheese; drizzle with vinaigrette. Serve with yogurt.

Beer Grilled
Steaks

Classic California Burgers

Makes 4 servings

- 2 tablespoons FRENCH'S® Honey Dijon Mustard
- 2 tablespoons mayonnaise
- 2 tablespoons sour cream
- 1 pound ground beef
- 2 tablespoons FRENCH'S® Worcestershire Sauce
- 1⅓ cups FRENCH'S® Cheddar or Original French Fried Onions, divided
- ½ teaspoon garlic salt
- ¼ teaspoon ground black pepper
- 4 hamburger rolls, split and toasted
- ½ small avocado, sliced
- ½ cup alfalfa sprouts

1. Combine mustard, mayonnaise and sour cream; set aside.

2. Combine beef, Worcestershire, ⅔ *cup* French Fried Onions and seasonings. Form into 4 patties. Grill over high heat until juices run clear (160°F internal temperature).

3. Place burgers on rolls. Top each with mustard sauce, avocado slices, sprouts and remaining onions, dividing evenly. Cover with top halves of rolls.

BBQ Cheese Burgers

Top each burger with 1 slice American cheese, 1 tablespoon barbecue sauce and 2 tablespoons French Fried Onions.

Pizza Burgers

Top each burger with pizza sauce, mozzarella cheese and French Fried Onions.

Garlic Grilled Beef Brochettes

Makes 4 servings

⅓ cup Caesar salad dressing

3 cloves garlic, minced

1 pound beef tenderloin tips or steaks, cut into 1½-inch pieces

1 small red onion, cut into ½-inch-thick wedges

1 large red or yellow bell pepper (or ½ of each), cut into 1-inch pieces

2 tablespoons chopped fresh thyme or rosemary

1. Prepare grill for direct cooking or preheat grill grid over campfire. Soak wooden skewers in water 20 minutes. Combine dressing and garlic in shallow dish. Add tenderloin, onion and bell pepper; toss to coat. Let stand 20 minutes.

2. Alternately thread meat and vegetables onto four long skewers. Brush any remaining marinade from dish over meat and vegetables.

3. Grill skewers, covered, over medium-high heat 5 minutes on each side. (Tenderloin will be pink in center and vegetables will be crisp-tender.) Top with thyme.

Steak Parmesan

Makes 2 servings

4 **cloves garlic, minced**

1 **tablespoon olive oil**

1 **tablespoon coarse salt**

1 **teaspoon black pepper**

2 **beef T-bone or Porterhouse steaks, cut 1 to 1¼ inch thick (about 2 pounds)**

¼ **cup grated Parmesan cheese**

1. Prepare grill for direct cooking or preheat grill grid over campfire. Combine garlic, oil, salt and pepper in small bowl; press into both sides of steaks. Let stand 15 minutes.

2. Place steaks on grid over medium-high heat. Cover; grill 14 to 19 minutes or until internal temperature reaches 145°F for medium-rare doneness, turning once.

3. Remove steaks to large cutting board; sprinkle with cheese. Tent with foil; let stand 5 minutes. Serve immediately.

Tip

For a smoky flavor, soak 2 cups hickory or oak wood chips in cold water to cover at least 30 minutes. Drain and scatter over hot coals before grilling. Makes 2 to 3 servings.

Western Barbecue Burgers with Beer Barbecue Sauce

Makes 4 servings

1½ **pounds ground beef**

1 **cup smokehouse-style barbecue sauce**

¼ **cup brown ale**

½ **teaspoon salt**

¼ **teaspoon black pepper**

1 **red onion, cut into ½-inch-thick slices**

4 **hamburger buns**

8 **slices thick-cut bacon, crisp-cooked**

Tomato slices

Lettuce leaves

1. Prepare grill for direct cooking or preheat grill grid over campfire. Shape beef into four patties, about ¾ inch thick.

2. Combine barbecue sauce, ale, salt and pepper in small saucepan. Bring to a boil; boil 1 minute. Set aside.

3. Grill burgers, covered, over medium-high heat 8 to 10 minutes or to desired doneness, turning occasionally. Grill onion 4 minutes or until softened and slightly charred, turning occasionally.

4. Serve burgers on buns with onion, bacon, barbecue sauce mixture, tomatoes and lettuce.

Bold and Zesty Beef Back Ribs

Makes 5 to 6 servings

5 pounds beef back ribs, cut into 3- or 4-rib pieces

Salt and black pepper

1 teaspoon vegetable oil

1 small onion, minced

2 cloves garlic, minced

1 cup ketchup

½ cup chili sauce

2 tablespoons lemon juice

1 tablespoon packed brown sugar

1 teaspoon hot pepper sauce

1. Place ribs in shallow pan; season with salt and black pepper. Refrigerate until ready to grill.

2. For sauce, heat oil in medium saucepan over medium heat. Add onion and garlic; cook and stir 5 minutes or until onion is tender. Stir in ketchup, chili sauce, lemon juice, brown sugar and hot pepper sauce. Reduce heat to medium-low. Cook 15 minutes, stirring occasionally.

3. Meanwhile, prepare grill for indirect cooking or preheat grill grid over campfire.

4. Place ribs on grid directly over drip pan. Baste ribs generously with half of sauce. Grill, covered, 45 to 60 minutes or until ribs are tender and browned, turning occasionally.

5. Bring remaining sauce to a boil over medium-high heat; boil 1 minute. Serve ribs with sauce.

Peppercorn Steaks

Makes 4 servings

2 tablespoons olive oil

1 to 2 teaspoons cracked pink or black peppercorns or ground black pepper

1 teaspoon dried herbs, such as rosemary or parsley

1 teaspoon minced garlic

4 boneless beef top loin (strip) or rib-eye steaks (6 ounces each)

¼ teaspoon salt

1. Combine oil, peppercorns, herbs and garlic in small bowl. Rub mixture on both sides of steaks. Place on plate; cover and refrigerate 30 to 60 minutes.

2. Prepare grill for direct cooking or preheat grill grid over campfire.

3. Grill steaks, uncovered, over medium heat 10 to 12 minutes for medium rare (145°F) to medium (160°F) or to desired doneness, turning once. Season with salt.

Ultimate Cheeseburgers

Makes 4 servings

1½ pounds ground beef

1½ teaspoons kosher salt *or* 1¼ teaspoons regular salt

½ teaspoon black pepper

4 sesame seed hamburger buns, split

4 slices American or Cheddar cheese

Optional toppings: sliced tomatoes, lettuce, sliced red onion and/or pickle or jalapeño slices

1. Shape beef into four patties slightly larger than size of buns. Combine salt and pepper in small bowl; sprinkle over both sides of patties. Make 1-inch-wide shallow indentation in center of each patty to discourage shrinkage.

2. Preheat grill to medium-high or preheat grill grid over campfire. Place patties on grid. Grill, covered, 2½ minutes or until browned on bottom. Turn; grill 2½ minutes for medium rare (145°F) or until burger feels soft when pressed in center with finger. Remove to plate. Place buns on grid, cut sides down, and grill 1 minute or until toasted.

3. Serve burgers on buns with desired toppings.

Peppercorn Steaks

Backyard Barbecue Burgers

Makes 6 servings

1½ **pounds ground beef**

5 **tablespoons barbecue sauce, divided**

1 **onion, cut into thick slices**

1 **tomato, sliced**

2 **tablespoons olive oil**

6 **Kaiser rolls, split**

6 **leaves green or red leaf lettuce**

1. Prepare grill for direct cooking or preheat grill grid over campfire. Combine beef and 2 tablespoons barbecue sauce in large bowl. Shape into six 1-inch-thick patties.

2. Grill patties, covered, over medium heat 8 to 10 minutes (or uncovered 13 to 15 minutes) to medium (160°F) or to desired doneness, turning occasionally. Brush both sides with remaining 3 tablespoons barbecue sauce during last 5 minutes of cooking.

3. Meanwhile, brush onion* and tomato slices with oil. Grill onion slices 10 minutes and tomato slices 2 to 3 minutes.

4. Just before serving, place rolls, cut side down, on grid; grill until lightly toasted. Serve burgers on rolls with tomato, onion and lettuce.

Onion slices may be cooked on the stovetop. Heat 2 tablespoons oil in large skillet over medium heat; add onions and cook 10 minutes or until tender and slightly browned, stirring frequently.

Spicy Smoked Beef Ribs

Makes 4 to 6 servings

- **4 wood chips for smoking**
- **4 to 6 pounds beef back ribs, cut into 3- to 4-rib portions**
- **Black pepper**
- **1⅓ cups barbecue sauce**
- **2 teaspoons hot pepper sauce or Szechuan chili sauce**
- **Beer, at room temperature, or hot water**

1. Soak wood chips in water at least 30 minutes; drain.

2. Spread ribs on large baking sheet; season with black pepper. Combine barbecue sauce and hot pepper sauce in small bowl. Brush ribs with half of sauce. Marinate in refrigerator 30 minutes to 1 hour.

3. Prepare grill for indirect cooking or preheat grill grid over campfire. Add soaked wood chips to fire. Place foil drip pan in center of grill. Fill pan half full with beer.

4. Place ribs on grid, meaty side up, directly above drip pan. Grill ribs, covered, over low heat 1 hour or until meat is tender, brushing remaining sauce over ribs 2 or 3 times during cooking. (If grill has thermometer, maintain cooking temperature at 250°F to 275°F. Add a few more coals as needed to maintain constant temperature.) Add more soaked wood chips after 30 minutes, if necessary.

Surf & Turf Kabobs

Makes 4 servings

1 **pound beef tenderloin, cut into 1¼-inch pieces**

12 **raw jumbo shrimp, peeled and deveined (with tails on)**

1 **medium onion, cut into 12 wedges**

1 **red or yellow bell pepper, cut into 1-inch pieces**

⅓ **cup butter, melted**

3 **tablespoons lemon juice**

3 **cloves garlic, minced**

2 **teaspoons paprika or smoked paprika**

½ **teaspoon salt**

¼ **teaspoon black pepper or ground red pepper**

Lemon wedges

1. Spray grid with nonstick cooking spray. Prepare grill for direct cooking or preheat grill grid over campfire. Alternately thread beef, shrimp, onion and bell pepper onto four 12-inch metal skewers. (Skewer shrimp through ends to form "C" shape for even cooking.)

2. Combine butter, lemon juice, garlic, paprika, salt and black pepper in small bowl; brush half of mixture over kabobs.

3. Grill kabobs over medium heat 5 minutes; turn and brush with remaining butter mixture. Grill 5 to 6 minutes or until shrimp are pink and opaque (beef will be medium rare (145°F) to medium (160°F) doneness). Serve with lemon wedges.

Tip

Be sure to purchase jumbo shrimp for this recipe. The shrimp and steak should be approximately the same size so they will cook evenly.

Pork Chops with
Pineapple Salsa,
page 104

Pleasing Pork

Sausage and Peppers

Makes 4 servings

½ cup olive oil

¼ cup red wine vinegar

2 tablespoons chopped fresh parsley

1 tablespoon dried oregano

2 cloves garlic, crushed

1 teaspoon salt

1 teaspoon black pepper

4 links hot or sweet Italian sausage

1 large onion, cut into rings

1 large bell pepper, cut into quarters

Horseradish-Mustard Spread (recipe follows)

1. Combine oil, vinegar, parsley, oregano, garlic, salt and black pepper in small bowl. Place sausage, onion and bell pepper in large resealable food storage bag; pour oil mixture over sausage and vegetables. Seal bag; turn to coat. Marinate in refrigerator 1 to 2 hours.

2. Prepare Horseradish-Mustard Spread; set aside. Prepare grill for direct cooking or preheat grill grid over campfire.

3. Remove sausage, onion and bell pepper from marinade; reserve marinade. Grill sausage, covered, over medium heat 5 minutes. Turn sausage and place onion and bell pepper on grid; brush with reserved marinade. Discard remaining marinade. Grill, covered, 5 minutes or until sausage is cooked through and vegetables are crisp-tender. Serve sausage and vegetables with Horseradish-Mustard Spread.

Horseradish-Mustard Spread

Makes about ¼ cup

3 tablespoons mayonnaise

1 tablespoon chopped fresh parsley

1 tablespoon prepared horseradish

1 tablespoon Dijon mustard

2 teaspoons garlic powder

1 teaspoon black pepper

Combine mayonnaise, parsley, horseradish, Dijon mustard, garlic powder and pepper in small bowl; stir to blend.

Thai Curry Coconut Pork Chops

Makes 6 servings

1 tablespoon vegetable oil

¼ cup *each* minced green onion and yellow onion

½ cup *Cattlemen's*® Golden Honey Barbecue Sauce

½ cup cream of coconut (not coconut milk)

¼ cup FRANK'S® RedHot® Original Cayenne Pepper Sauce

2 teaspoons grated peeled ginger root

½ teaspoon curry powder

¼ cup heavy cream

6 rib cut bone-in pork chops, cut 1-inch thick, seasoned with salt and pepper to taste

1. Prepare Thai Curry Coconut Sauce: Heat oil in small saucepan; sauté onions just until tender. Add barbecue sauce, cream of coconut, **FRANK'S® RedHot®** *Original Cayenne Pepper Sauce*, ginger and curry powder. Simmer 5 minutes until slightly thickened. Transfer ¾ cup sauce to bowl for basting. Add cream to remaining sauce. Simmer 3 minutes; keep warm.

2. Grill chops over medium direct heat 25 minutes or until no longer pink near bone, basting with chile sauce mixture during last 10 minutes of cooking.

3. Arrange chops on serving platter. Serve with Thai Curry Coconut Sauce and, if desired, steamed jasmine rice.

Serving Suggestion

For a colorful presentation, toss cooked rice with minced red onion and parsley.

Grilled Pork Fajitas with Mango and Salsa Verde

Makes 4 servings

2 cloves garlic, crushed

2 teaspoons chili powder

½ teaspoon ground cumin

½ teaspoon ground coriander

12 ounces pork tenderloin, trimmed of fat

1 medium red onion, cut into ½-inch rings

1 mango, peeled and cut into ½-inch pieces

8 (6-inch) flour tortillas, warmed

½ cup salsa verde

1. Spray grid with nonstick cooking spray. Prepare grill for direct cooking or preheat grill grid over campfire.

2. Combine garlic, chili powder, cumin and coriander in small bowl. Rub evenly onto pork.

3. Grill pork over medium-high heat 12 to 16 minutes or until thermometer registers 155°F for medium doneness, turning occasionally. During last 8 minutes of grilling, grill onion until tender, turning occasionally.

4. Remove onion to small bowl. Remove pork to large cutting board; tent loosely with foil. Let stand 5 to 10 minutes before slicing into ½-inch strips.

5. Arrange pork, onion and mango on tortillas. Spoon evenly with salsa verde. Fold bottom 3 inches of each tortilla up over filling; roll up to enclose filling.

Beer-Brined Grilled Pork Chops

Makes 4 servings

- 1 **bottle (12 ounces) dark beer**
- ¼ **cup packed dark brown sugar**
- 1 **tablespoon salt**
- 1 **tablespoon chili powder**
- 2 **cloves garlic, minced**
- 3 **cups ice water**
- 4 **pork chops (1 inch thick)**
- **Grilled Rosemary Potatoes (recipe follows)**

1. Whisk beer, brown sugar, salt, chili powder and garlic in medium bowl until salt is dissolved. Add ice water and stir until ice melts. Add pork chops; place medium plate on top to keep chops submerged in brine. Refrigerate 3 to 4 hours.

2. Prepare grill for direct cooking or preheat grill grid over campfire. Drain pork chops and pat dry with paper towels. Prepare Grilled Rosemary Potatoes. Grill pork chops, covered, over medium heat 10 to 12 minutes. Serve with potatoes.

Tip

Brining adds flavor and moisture to meats. Be sure that your pork chops have not been injected with a sodium solution (check the package label) or they could end up too salty.

Grilled Rosemary Potatoes

Place 4 quartered potatoes, 1 cup sliced bell pepper, ¼ cup chopped onion, 2 teaspoons chopped fresh rosemary and 1 teaspoon red pepper flakes on a 13×9-inch piece of foil. Toss mixture on foil; top with an additional 13×9-inch piece of foil. Seal edges of foil pieces together to make a packet. Grill 12 to 15 minutes or until potatoes are tender. Makes 4 servings.

Brats 'n' Beer

Makes 4 servings

1 **can (12 ounces) beer (not dark-colored)**

4 **bratwurst (about 1 pound)**

1 **sweet or Spanish onion, thinly sliced and separated into rings**

1 **tablespoon olive oil**

¼ **teaspoon salt**

¼ **teaspoon black pepper**

4 **sausage rolls**

1. Prepare grill for direct cooking or preheat grill grid over campfire.

2. Pour beer into medium heavy saucepan with ovenproof handle. Place saucepan on grid. Pierce bratwurst with knife; add to beer. Simmer 15 minutes, turning once.

3. Place onion rings on sheet of heavy-duty foil. Drizzle with oil; sprinkle with salt and pepper. Fold sides of foil over rings to enclose. Place packets on grid. Grill over medium heat 10 minutes or until tender.

4. Transfer bratwurst to grid. Remove saucepan from grid; discard beer. Grill bratwurst 10 minutes or until browned and cooked through, turning once. Place bratwurst in rolls. Top with onion rings.

Tailgate Pizza

Makes 4 servings

1 cup pizza sauce

4 individual (8-inch) prepared pizza crusts

3 cups (12 ounces) shredded mozzarella cheese or Italian cheese blend

8 ounces bulk Italian sausage, cooked, drained (1½ cups)

2 ounces sliced pepperoni

1 small red onion, thinly sliced

1 small red bell pepper, thinly sliced into rings

1 small green bell pepper, thinly sliced into rings

Red pepper flakes (optional)

1. Place all ingredients in individual bowls for transporting to the grill.

2. Prepare grill for indirect cooking or preheat grill grid over campfire.

3. To assemble pizzas, spread pizza sauce over crusts; top with cheese, sausage, pepperoni, onion, bell peppers and red pepper flakes, if desired. Grill pizzas, covered, over low heat 8 to 10 minutes or until cheese is melted and crust is golden brown.

Pork Chops with Pineapple Salsa

Makes 4 servings

¾ cup teriyaki marinade, divided

4 boneless pork loin chops, ¾-inch thick

1 can (20 oz.) DOLE® Pineapple Chunks, drained, diced

⅓ cup finely chopped red onion

½ small red bell pepper, finely chopped

2 tablespoons chopped fresh cilantro

1 medium jalapeño pepper, seeded, finely chopped (optional)

- **Pour** ¼ cup teriyaki marinade over pork chops in a sealable plastic bag. Refrigerate and marinate for 30 minutes.

- **Combine** ¼ cup teriyaki marinade with pineapple chunks, red onion, bell pepper, cilantro and jalapeño pepper. Let stand at room temperature up to 1 hour.

- **Remove** pork chops from teriyaki marinade, discarding marinade. Grill or broil pork chops 10 to 15 minutes turning and brushing occasionally with remaining ¼ cup teriyaki marinade or until pork reaches internal temperature of 145°F. Discard any remaining marinade. Serve chops with pineapple salsa.

Grilled Pork in Pita

Makes 6 servings

¾ **cup Pace® Picante Sauce**

½ **cup plain yogurt**

1 **teaspoon lime juice**

¼ **teaspoon garlic powder or 2 cloves garlic, minced**

1 **pound boneless pork chops, ¾-inch thick**

6 **pita breads (6-inch), warmed**

1 **cup shredded lettuce**

1 **medium green onion, sliced (about 2 tablespoons)**

1. Stir **3 tablespoons** picante sauce, yogurt and lime juice in a small bowl. Cover and refrigerate until ready to serve. Stir the remaining picante sauce and garlic powder in a small bowl.

2. Lightly oil the grill rack and heat the grill to medium-high. Grill the pork for 15 minutes or until it's cooked through, turning and brushing often with the picante sauce mixture. Discard any remaining picante sauce mixture.

3. Slice the pork into thin strips. Divide the pork among the pita breads. Top with the yogurt mixture, lettuce and green onion. Fold the pitas around the filling.

Kitchen Tip

To warm the pita breads, wrap them in a plain paper towel. Microwave on HIGH for 1 minute or until they're warm.

Baby Back Barbecue Ribs

Makes 5 to 6 servings

2 sheets (18×24 inches each) REYNOLDS WRAP® Non-Stick Foil

3 pounds baby back pork ribs

1 tablespoon packed brown sugar

1 tablespoon paprika

2 teaspoons garlic powder

1½ teaspoons pepper

½ cup water or 6 to 8 ice cubes, divided

1½ cups barbecue sauce

PREHEAT grill to medium.

CENTER half of ribs on each sheet of REYNOLDS WRAP® Non-Stick. Combine brown sugar and spices; rub over ribs, turning to coat evenly.

BRING up foil sides. Double fold top and one end to seal packet. Through open end, add ¼ cup of water or 3 to 4 ice cubes. Double fold remaining end, leaving room for heat circulation inside. Repeat to make two packets.

GRILL for 45 to 60 minutes in covered grill. Remove ribs from foil; place ribs on grill.

BRUSH ribs with barbecue sauce. Continue grilling 10 to 15 minutes, brushing with sauce and turning every 5 minutes.

Cuban Garlic & Lime Pork Chops

Makes 4 servings

4 **boneless pork top loin chops, ¾ inch thick (about 1½ pounds)**

2 **tablespoons olive oil**

2 **tablespoons lime juice**

2 **tablespoons orange juice**

2 **teaspoons minced garlic**

½ **teaspoon salt, divided**

½ **teaspoon red pepper flakes**

Salsa

2 **small seedless oranges, peeled and chopped**

1 **medium cucumber, peeled, seeded and chopped**

2 **tablespoons chopped onion**

2 **tablespoons chopped fresh cilantro**

1. Place pork in large resealable food storage bag. Add oil, lime juice, orange juice, garlic, ¼ teaspoon salt and red pepper flakes. Seal bag; turn to coat. Marinate in refrigerator at least 1 hour or overnight.

2. Combine oranges, cucumber, onion and cilantro in medium bowl; toss gently. Cover and refrigerate 1 hour or overnight. Add remaining ¼ teaspoon salt just before serving.

3. Prepare grill for direct cooking or preheat grill grid over campfire. Remove pork from marinade; discard marinade. Grill pork over medium heat 6 to 8 minutes on each side or until pork is no longer pink in center. Serve with salsa.

Pepperoni Pizza Sandwich

Makes 1 serving

- **2 slices white sandwich bread**
- **2 tablespoons prepared pizza sauce**
- **3 tablespoons mozzarella cheese**
- **5 slices pepperoni**
- **2 tablespoons butter**

1. Spread 1 bread slice with pizza sauce; top with cheese, pepperoni and 1 bread slice. Place 1 tablespoon butter in pie iron. Add sandwich; top with 1 tablespoon butter. Close pie iron.

2. Hold pie iron level over medium coals of campfire 6 minutes or until golden brown on each side, turning once. Remove to heatproof surface; carefully remove sandwich to serving plate.

Toasted Cheese Sandwich

Layer 1 tablespoon butter, 1 bread slice, your favorite cheese(s), 1 bread slice and 1 tablespoon butter in pie iron. Close pi e iron. Follow method step 2 as directed. Makes 1 serving.

Thai-Style Pork Kabobs

Makes 4 servings

⅓ cup soy sauce

2 tablespoons fresh lime juice

2 tablespoons water

2 teaspoons hot chili oil*

2 cloves garlic, minced

1 teaspoon minced fresh ginger

12 ounces pork tenderloin

1 red or yellow bell pepper, cut into ½-inch pieces

1 red or sweet onion, cut into ½-inch pieces

2 cups hot cooked rice

If hot chili oil is not available, combine 2 teaspoons vegetable oil and ½ teaspoon red pepper flakes in small microwavable bowl. Microwave on HIGH 30 to 45 seconds. Let stand 5 minutes to allow flavors to develop.

1. Whisk soy sauce, lime juice, water, chili oil, garlic and ginger in medium bowl until well blended. Reserve ⅓ cup for dipping sauce. Soak eight 8- to 10-inch wooden skewers in water 20 minutes.

2. Cut pork tenderloin into ½-inch strips. Add to remaining soy sauce mixture; toss to coat evenly. Cover; refrigerate at least 30 minutes or up to 2 hours, turning once.

3. Spray grid with nonstick cooking spray. Prepare grill for direct cooking or preheat grill grid over campfire.

4. Remove pork from marinade; discard marinade. Alternately thread pork strips, bell pepper and onion onto skewers.

5. Grill, covered, over medium heat 6 to 8 minutes or until pork is barely pink in center, turning halfway through grilling time.

6. Serve with rice and reserved dipping sauce.

Maple Francheezies

Makes 4 servings

Mustard Spread (recipe follows)

¼ cup maple syrup

2 teaspoons garlic powder

1 teaspoon black pepper

½ teaspoon ground nutmeg

4 slices bacon

4 jumbo hot dogs

4 hot dog buns, split

½ cup (2 ounces) shredded Cheddar cheese

1. Prepare Mustard Spread; set aside.

2. Prepare grill for direct cooking or preheat grill grid over campfire.

3. Combine maple syrup, garlic powder, pepper and nutmeg in small bowl. Brush syrup mixture onto bacon slices. Wrap 1 slice bacon around each hot dog.

4. Brush hot dogs with remaining syrup mixture. Grill hot dogs, covered, over medium-high heat 8 minutes or until bacon is crisp and hot dogs are heated through, turning once. Place hot dogs in buns; top with Mustard Spread and cheese.

Mustard Spread

Makes about ¾ cup

½ cup yellow mustard

1 tablespoon finely chopped onion

1 tablespoon diced tomato

1 tablespoon chopped fresh parsley

1 teaspoon garlic powder

½ teaspoon black pepper

Combine mustard, onion, tomato, parsley, garlic powder and pepper in small bowl; stir to blend.

Grilled Pork Chops with Lager Barbecue Sauce

Makes 4 servings

1 cup lager

⅓ cup maple syrup

3 tablespoons molasses

1 teaspoon Mexican-style hot chili powder

4 bone-in center-cut pork chops, 1 inch thick (2 to 2¼ pounds)

Lager Barbecue Sauce (recipe follows)

¾ teaspoon salt

¼ teaspoon black pepper

1. Combine lager, maple syrup, molasses, chili powder and pork chops in large resealable food storage bag. Marinate in refrigerator 2 hours, turning occasionally. Prepare Lager Barbecue Sauce.

2. Prepare grill for direct cooking or preheat grill grid over campfire. Oil grid.

3. Remove pork chops from marinade; discard marinade. Sprinkle with salt and pepper. Grill over medium-high heat 6 to 7 minutes per side or until 160°F. Serve with Lager Barbecue Sauce.

Lager Barbecue Sauce

Makes about ½ cup

½ cup lager

⅓ cup ketchup

3 tablespoons maple syrup

2 tablespoons finely chopped onion

1 tablespoon molasses

1 tablespoon cider vinegar

½ teaspoon Mexican-style hot chili powder

Combine lager, ketchup, maple syrup, onion, molasses, vinegar and chili powder in small saucepan over medium heat. Bring to a gentle simmer and cook, stirring occasionally, 10 to 12 minutes or until slightly thickened.

Pork and Plum Kabobs

Makes 4 servings

¾ **pound boneless pork loin chops (1 inch thick), trimmed and cut into 1-inch pieces**

1½ **teaspoons ground cumin**

½ **teaspoon ground cinnamon**

¼ **teaspoon salt**

¼ **teaspoon garlic powder**

¼ **teaspoon ground red pepper**

¼ **cup sliced green onions**

¼ **cup raspberry fruit spread**

1 **tablespoon orange juice**

3 **plums or nectarines, pitted and cut into wedges**

1. Soak eight wooden skewers in water 20 minutes. Place pork in large resealable food storage bag. Combine cumin, cinnamon, salt, garlic powder and ground red pepper in small bowl; pour over pork. Seal bag; shake to coat pork with spices.

2. Combine green onions, fruit spread and orange juice in small bowl; set aside.

3. Prepare grill for direct cooking or preheat grill grid over campfire. Alternately thread pork and plum wedges onto skewers. Grill kabobs over medium heat 12 to 14 minutes or until pork is cooked through, turning once. Brush frequently with raspberry mixture during last 5 minutes of grilling.

Serving Suggestion

A crisp, cool salad makes a great accompaniment to these sweet grilled kabobs.

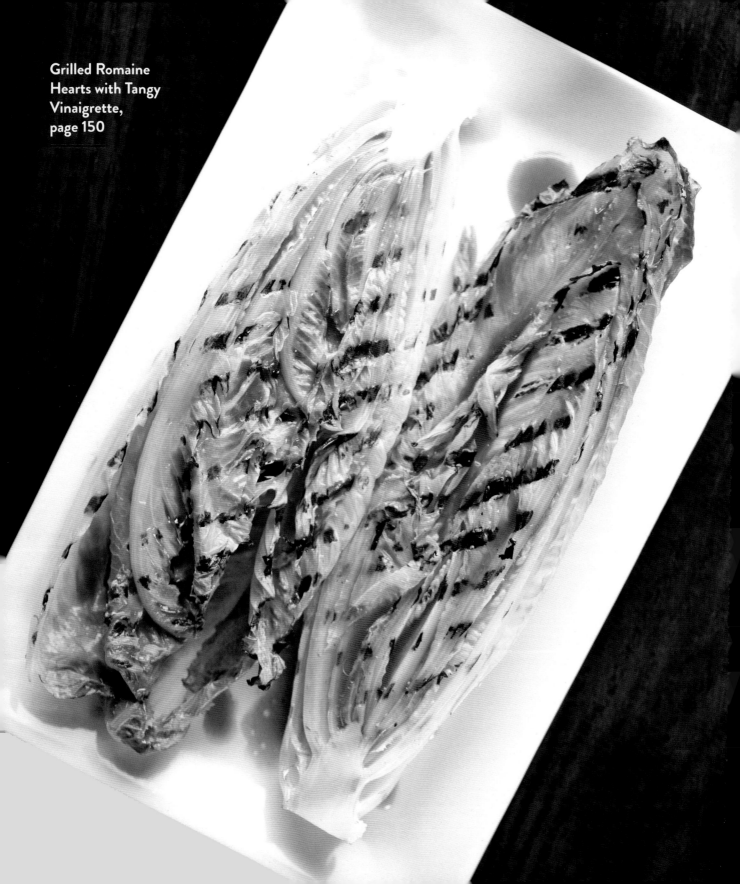

Grilled Romaine
Hearts with Tangy
Vinaigrette,
page 150

Sides & Salads

Jamaican Grilled Sweet Potatoes

Makes 6 servings

2 large sweet potatoes or yams (about 1½ pounds)

3 tablespoons packed brown sugar

3 tablespoons melted butter, divided

1 teaspoon ground ginger

1 tablespoon chopped fresh cilantro

2 teaspoons dark rum

1. Pierce potatoes in several places with fork. Place on paper towel in microwave. Microwave on HIGH 5 to 6 minutes or until crisp-tender, rotating one-fourth turn halfway through cooking time. Let stand 10 minutes. Diagonally slice potatoes into ¾-inch slices.

2. Prepare grill for direct cooking or preheat grill grid over campfire. Combine brown sugar, 1 tablespoon melted butter and ginger in small bowl; mix well. Stir in cilantro and rum; set aside. Lightly brush one side of each potato slice with half of remaining melted butter.

3. Grill sweet potato slices, butter side down, on covered grill over medium heat 4 to 6 minutes or until grill marked. Brush tops with remaining melted butter. Turn; grill 3 to 5 minutes or until grill marked. To serve, spoon rum mixture equally over potato slices.

Grilled Brussels Sprouts with Pancetta

Makes 4 servings

1 pound Brussels sprouts (about 20), stems and loose leaves removed

1 tablespoon olive oil, divided

1 teaspoon minced garlic

¼ teaspoon salt

⅛ teaspoon black pepper

1 ounce pancetta, diced

Lemon wedges (optional)

1. Prepare grill for direct cooking or preheat grill grid over campfire. Soak wooden skewers in water 20 minutes. Microwave Brussels sprouts in large microwavable dish on HIGH 4 to 5 minutes. Let stand until cool enough to handle.

2. Combine 2 teaspoons oil, garlic, salt and pepper in large bowl. Add Brussels sprouts; toss to coat. Thread 5 Brussels sprouts onto each skewer.

3. Grill skewers, covered, over medium heat 5 minutes. Turn skewers and grill 5 minutes.

4. Heat remaining 1 teaspoon oil in large skillet over medium heat. Add pancetta; cook and stir 5 minutes or until crisp.

5. Remove Brussels sprouts from skewers to skillet; toss to coat. Serve with lemon wedges, if desired.

Tomato Watermelon Salad

Makes 4 servings

Dressing

- ¼ **cup extra virgin olive oil**
- 2 **tablespoons fresh lemon juice**
- ½ **teaspoon honey**
- ½ **teaspoon salt**
- ⅛ **teaspoon black pepper**

Salad

- 2 **large heirloom tomatoes (about 10 ounces each), cut into 6 slices each**
- 2 **cups cubed watermelon (about 12 ounces)**
- ¼ **cup thinly sliced red onion rings**
- ¼ **cup crumbled feta cheese**
- **Chopped fresh chervil or parsley (optional)**

1. For dressing, whisk oil, lemon juice, honey, salt and pepper in small bowl until well blended.

2. For salad, arrange tomato slices on four salad plates. Top with watermelon and onion; sprinkle with cheese. Drizzle with dressing; garnish with chervil.

Farmers' Market Potato Salad

Makes 6 servings

Pickled Red Onions (recipe follows)

2 cups cubed assorted potatoes (purple, baby red, Yukon Gold and/or a combination)

1 cup fresh green beans, cut into 1-inch pieces

2 tablespoons plain nonfat Greek yogurt

2 tablespoons white wine vinegar

2 tablespoons olive oil

1 tablespoon spicy mustard

1 teaspoon salt

1. Prepare Pickled Red Onions.

2. Bring large saucepan of water to a boil. Add potatoes; cook 5 to 8 minutes or until fork-tender.* Add green beans during last 4 minutes of cooking time. Drain potatoes and green beans.

3. Whisk yogurt, vinegar, oil, mustard and salt in large bowl until smooth and well blended.

4. Add potatoes, green beans and Pickled Red Onions to dressing; toss gently to coat. Cover; refrigerate at least 1 hour before serving to allow flavors to develop.

Some potatoes may take longer to cook than others. Remove individual potatoes to large bowl using slotted spoon when fork-tender.

Pickled Red Onions

Makes about ½ cup

½ cup thinly sliced red onion

¼ cup white wine vinegar

2 tablespoons water

1 teaspoon sugar

½ teaspoon salt

Combine all ingredients in large glass jar. Seal jar; shake well. Refrigerate at least 1 hour or up to 1 week.

Spicy Grilled Corn

Makes 4 servings

2 tablespoons butter, softened

1 tablespoon chopped fresh parsley

2 teaspoons lemon juice

½ teaspoon salt

½ teaspoon black pepper

½ teaspoon red pepper flakes

4 ears corn, husks and silks removed

1. Prepare grill for direct cooking or preheat grill grid over campfire. Combine butter, parsley, lemon juice, salt, black pepper and red pepper flakes in small bowl. Brush mixture evenly over corn.

2. Place two sheets of foil (about 12×18 inches each) on work surface; center 2 ears of corn on each piece of foil. Bring up sides of foil; fold over top and edges to seal packets.

3. Grill packets, covered, over medium-high heat 15 minutes or until corn is tender, turning once.

Classic Italian Pasta Salad

Makes 8 side-dish servings

8 ounces rotelle or spiral pasta, cooked and drained

2½ cups assorted cut-up fresh vegetables (broccoli, carrots, tomatoes, bell peppers and onions)

½ cup cubed Cheddar or mozzarella cheese

⅓ cup sliced pitted ripe olives (optional)

1 cup WISH-BONE® Italian Dressing

Combine all ingredients except WISH-BONE® Italian Dressing in large bowl. Add Dressing; toss well. Serve chilled or at room temperature.

Tip

If preparing a day ahead, refrigerate, then stir in ¼ cup additional WISH-BONE® Dressing before serving.

Variation

For a Creamy Italian Pasta Salad, substitute ½ cup HELLMANN'S® or BEST FOODS® Real Mayonnaise for ½ cup WISH-BONE® Italian Dressing.

Spicy Grilled Corn

Fruit Salad with Creamy Banana Dressing

Makes 8 servings

- 2 cups fresh pineapple chunks
- 1 cup cantaloupe cubes
- 1 cup honeydew melon cubes
- 1 cup fresh blackberries
- 1 cup sliced fresh strawberries
- 1 cup seedless red grapes
- 1 medium apple, diced
- 2 medium ripe bananas, sliced
- ½ cup vanilla nonfat Greek yogurt
- 2 tablespoons honey
- 1 tablespoon fresh lemon juice
- ¼ teaspoon ground nutmeg

1. Combine pineapple, cantaloupe, honeydew, blackberries, strawberries, grapes and apple in large bowl; mix gently.

2. Combine bananas, yogurt, honey, lemon juice and nutmeg in blender or food processor; blend until smooth.

3. Pour dressing over fruit mixture; gently toss to coat. Serve immediately.

Greek Pasta Salad in a Jar

Makes 6 servings

Pasta Salad

6 cups cooked regular or multigrain rotini pasta

1½ cups diced cucumber

1 cup diced tomatoes (about 2 medium)

1 cup diced green bell pepper (about 1 medium)

1 package (4 ounces) crumbled feta cheese

12 medium pitted black olives, sliced

¼ cup chopped fresh dill

Dressing

¼ cup olive oil

¼ cup lemon juice

¼ teaspoon salt

¼ teaspoon dried oregano

⅛ teaspoon black pepper

1. For pasta salad, combine pasta, cucumber, tomatoes, bell pepper, cheese, olives and dill in large bowl; toss to blend.

2. For dressing, combine oil, lemon juice, salt, oregano and black pepper in small bowl; stir to blend. Pour over pasta; toss well to coat.

3. If desired, spoon about 2 cups pasta salad into each of six (1-pint) resealable jars. Seal jars. Refrigerate until ready to serve.

Szechuan Grilled Mushrooms

Makes 4 servings

1 **pound large mushrooms**

2 **tablespoons soy sauce**

2 **teaspoons peanut or vegetable oil**

1 **teaspoon dark sesame oil**

1 **clove garlic, minced**

½ **teaspoon crushed Szechuan peppercorns or red pepper flakes**

1. Soak wooden skewers in water 20 minutes.

2. Meanwhile, place mushrooms in large resealable food storage bag. Combine soy sauce, peanut oil, sesame oil, garlic and Szechuan peppercorns in small bowl; pour over mushrooms. Seal bag; turn to coat. Marinate at room temperature 15 minutes.

3. Prepare grill for direct cooking or preheat grill grid over campfire. Thread mushrooms onto skewers. Reserve marinade.

4. Grill mushrooms over medium-high heat 5 inches from heat 10 minutes or until lightly browned, turning once. Serve immediately with reserved marinade.

Variation

For Szechuan-Grilled Mushrooms and Onions, add 4 green onions, cut into 1½-inch pieces, to marinade. Alternately thread onto skewers with mushrooms. Proceed as directed in step 4.

Ramen Antipasti Salad

Makes 6 servings

- **1 can (about 14 ounces) whole artichoke hearts, drained and liquid reserved**
- **1 package (3 ounces) chicken-flavored ramen noodles, coarsely crumbled**
- **1 cup grape tomatoes, quartered**
- **4 ounces small fresh mozzarella balls**
- **2 ounces hard salami, thinly sliced**
- **½ cup pitted kalamata olives**
- **¼ cup diced red onion**
- **¼ cup fresh basil _or_ 1 tablespoon dried basil**
- **¼ cup extra virgin olive oil**
- **2 tablespoons cider vinegar**
- **1 medium clove garlic, minced**
- **½ teaspoon black pepper**
- **¼ teaspoon red pepper flakes (optional)**

1. Combine reserved artichoke liquid and ramen seasoning packet in medium saucepan; bring to a boil over high heat. Add noodles; cook over medium heat 2 to 3 minutes or just until tender. (Noodles should absorb most of liquid.) Spread noodles in thin layer on rimmed plate to cool 10 minutes. Discard any excess cooking liquid.

2. Cut artichokes into halves; place in large bowl. Add tomatoes, mozzarella, salami, olives, onion, basil, oil, vinegar, garlic, black pepper and red pepper flakes, if desired; stir gently.

3. Add noodles to salad; stir gently to coat.

Grilled Sesame Asparagus

Makes 4 servings

1 **pound medium asparagus spears (about 20), trimmed**

1 **tablespoon sesame seeds**

2 **to 3 teaspoons balsamic vinegar**

¼ **teaspoon salt**

¼ **teaspoon black pepper**

1. Spray grid with nonstick cooking spray. Prepare grill for direct cooking or preheat grill grid over campfire.

2. Place asparagus on baking sheet; spray lightly with cooking spray. Sprinkle with sesame seeds, rolling to coat.

3. Place asparagus on grid. Grill, uncovered, over medium heat 4 to 6 minutes or until asparagus begins to brown, turning once.

4. Remove asparagus to serving dish. Sprinkle with vinegar, salt and pepper.

Best Ever Barbecued Beans

Makes 6 to 8 servings

3 **thick or 5 thin slices bacon, diced**

1 **medium onion, chopped**

1 **green bell pepper, diced**

¼ **cup ketchup**

2 **tablespoons molasses**

2 **tablespoons packed light brown sugar**

2 **tablespoons coarse-grain or spicy brown mustard**

2 **cans (15 or 16 ounces each) navy or great northern beans, drained**

1. Cook bacon in large saucepan over medium heat 3 minutes. Add onion; cook 5 minutes, stirring occasionally. Stir in bell pepper; cook 3 minutes. Add ketchup, molasses, brown sugar and mustard; mix well. Add beans; mix well. Cover; simmer over medium-low heat 20 minutes.

2. Reheat in covered pot on grill or over campfire until heated through.

Grilled Sesame Asparagus

Fire-Roasted Hasselback Potatoes

Makes 6 servings

6 large baking potatoes

Olive oil

2 tablespoons garlic powder

1 tablespoon salt

2 teaspoons black pepper

1. Cut each potato crosswise at ¼-inch-thick slices, leaving about ¼ inch at bottom. Rub each potato with oil, garlic powder, salt and pepper, making sure oil and seasonings get inside potato slits. Place each potato on 6×6-inch piece of foil. Roll up to seal.

2. Place potatoes directly in medium coals of campfire. Cook 40 minutes or until potatoes are softened. Remove to heatproof surface using large tongs. Cool potatoes until cool enough to handle.

Black Bean & Corn Ranch Salad

Makes 5 servings

½ cup WISH-BONE® Light Ranch Dressing

1 can (about 15 ounces) reduced-sodium black beans, rinsed and drained

1 can (11 ounces) whole kernel corn or mexi-corn, drained

1 cup quartered grape or cherry tomatoes

½ cup chopped red onion

2 tablespoons chopped fresh cilantro

Hot pepper sauce (optional)

Combine all ingredients in medium bowl. Serve chilled or at room temperature.

Fire-Roasted
Hasselback Potatoes

Grilled Peach Salad

Makes 4 servings

4 **peaches, halved and pitted**

1 **container (16 ounces) arugula**

1 **block (8 ounces) feta cheese, cut into 1-inch pieces**

1 **pint cherry tomatoes, halved (optional)**

Prepared balsamic vinaigrette

1. Prepare grill for direct cooking over medium-high heat or preheat grill grid over campfire. Spray grid with nonstick cooking spray.

2. Place peaches, cut sides down, on prepared grill. Grill, covered, 2 to 3 minutes. Turn over; grill 2 to 3 minutes or until peaches begin to soften. Remove to plate; let stand to cool slightly. Cut into wedges.

3. Divide arugula, cheese and tomatoes, if desired, evenly among four plates; top with peaches and vinaigrette.

Picnic Potato Salad

Makes 6 servings

- **4 large potatoes**
- **¾ cup mayonnaise**
- **1 tablespoon yellow mustard**
- **2 tablespoons minced fresh parsley**
- **⅓ cup chopped dill pickle**
- **⅓ cup chopped red onion**
- **2 hard-cooked eggs, chopped**
- **Salt and black pepper (optional)**

1. Place potatoes in large saucepan; add enough water to cover. Bring to a boil over medium-high heat. Cook 5 to 7 minutes or until potatoes are fork-tender but not mushy. Drain and cool slightly.

2. When cool enough to handle, cut potatoes into 1-inch cubes. Whisk mayonnaise, mustard and parsley in large bowl. Stir in pickle and onion. Gently fold in potatoes and eggs. Season with salt and pepper, if desired.

Grilled Romaine Hearts with Tangy Vinaigrette

Makes 6 servings, plus 1 quart vinaigrette

Tangy Vinaigrette

- **3 cups cola**
- **⅓ cup white vinegar**
- **⅓ cup canola oil**
- **¼ cup sugar**
- **1 teaspoon salt**
- **½ teaspoon onion powder**
- **½ teaspoon garlic powder**
- **3 tablespoons ketchup**
- **1 tablespoon balsamic vinegar**
- **⅛ teaspoon black pepper**
- **2 tablespoons honey mustard**

Romaine Hearts

- **6 romaine hearts**
- **¼ to ½ cup olive oil**
- **Salt and black pepper**

1. Combine cola, white vinegar, canola oil, sugar, 1 teaspoon salt, onion powder, garlic powder, ketchup, balsamic vinegar, ⅛ teaspoon pepper and mustard in medium bowl; set aside.

2. Prepare grill for direct cooking over medium-high heat. Cut romaine hearts in half lengthwise, drizzle with olive oil and sprinkle generously with salt and pepper.

3. Grill about 2 minutes on each side, until lightly charred and wilted.

4. Drizzle with Tangy Vinaigrette and serve. Refrigerate remaining vinaigrette for future use.

Hot and Spicy Fruit Salad

Makes 6 servings

⅓ cup orange juice

3 tablespoons lime juice

3 tablespoons minced fresh mint, basil or cilantro, plus additional for garnish

2 jalapeño peppers, seeded, minced

1 tablespoon honey

½ small honeydew melon, cut into cubes

1 ripe large papaya, peeled, seeded, cubed

1 pint fresh strawberries, stemmed, halved

1 can (8 ounces) pineapple chunks, drained

1. Blend orange juice, lime juice, 3 tablespoons mint, jalapeño peppers and honey in small bowl.

2. Combine melon, papaya, strawberries and pineapple in large bowl. Pour orange juice mixture over fruit; toss gently until well blended.

3. Serve immediately or cover and refrigerate up to 3 hours. Garnish with additional fresh mint.

Roasted Sweet Potatoes

Makes 6 servings

6 sweet potatoes

Vegetable oil

Optional toppings: marshmallows, ground cinnamon, sugar and/or butter

1. Rub each potato with oil. Place each potato on 6×6-inch piece of foil. Roll up to seal.

2. Place potatoes directly in medium coals. Cook 25 minutes or until potatoes are softened. Remove to heatproof surface using large tongs. Cool potatoes until cool enough to handle. Top as desired.

Grilled Cajun Potato Wedges

Makes 4 to 6 servings

3 large unpeeled russet potatoes, washed and scrubbed (about 2¼ pounds)

¼ cup olive oil

2 cloves garlic, minced

1 teaspoon salt

1 teaspoon paprika

½ teaspoon dried thyme

½ teaspoon dried oregano

¼ teaspoon black pepper

⅛ to ¼ teaspoon ground red pepper

2 cups mesquite chips

1. Prepare grill for direct cooking or preheat grill grid over campfire. Preheat oven to 425°F.

2. Cut potatoes in half lengthwise; then cut each half lengthwise into four wedges. Place potatoes in large bowl. Add oil and garlic; toss to coat well.

3. Combine salt, paprika, thyme, oregano, black pepper and ground red pepper in small bowl. Sprinkle over potatoes; toss to coat well. Place potato wedges in single layer in shallow roasting pan. (Reserve remaining oil mixture left in large bowl.) Bake 20 minutes.

4. Meanwhile, cover mesquite chips with cold water; soak 20 minutes. Drain mesquite chips; sprinkle over coals. Place potato wedges on their sides on grid. Grill potato wedges, covered, over medium heat 15 to 20 minutes or until potatoes are browned and fork-tender, brushing with reserved oil mixture halfway through grilling time and turning once with tongs.

Roasted
Sweet Potatoes

Individual Fruit Pie,
page 164

Desserts & Drinks

Cantarito

Makes 1 serving

Lime wedge

Coarse salt

1½ ounces tequila

½ ounce lime juice

½ ounce lemon juice

½ ounce orange juice

Grapefruit soda

Lime, lemon and/or orange wedges

Rub rim of Collins glass with lime wedge; dip in salt. Fill glass with ice; add tequila, lime juice, lemon juice and orange juice. Top with grapefruit soda; stir until blended. Garnish with citrus wedges.

Note

In Mexico, Cantaritos are typically served in salt-rimmed clay pots.

Margarita Pops

Makes 8 pops

2 cups water

⅔ cup fresh lime juice (2 to 3 limes)

½ cup tequila

¼ cup sugar

2 tablespoons Triple Sec or orange liqueur

8 (2-ounce) plastic or paper cups

8 pop sticks

Coarse salt

1. Combine water, lime juice, tequila, sugar and Triple Sec in small saucepan; bring to a boil. Boil 1 minute or until sugar is dissolved, stirring constantly. Remove from heat. Cool to room temperature.

2. Pour mixture into cups. Cover top of each cup with small piece of foil. Freeze 2 hours.

3. Insert sticks through center of foil. Freeze 3 hours or until firm.

4. Remove foil; gently twist frozen pops out of plastic cups or peel away paper cups.

5. Spread coarse salt on small plate. Roll pops in coarse salt. Serve immediately or place in plastic cups and return to freezer until ready to serve.

Cantarito

Poked S'mores Cake

Makes 12 to 15 servings

1 **package (about 15 ounces) chocolate cake mix, plus ingredients to prepare mix**

½ **jar marshmallow creme**

¾ **cup plus 1 tablespoon whipping cream, divided**

2 **cups semisweet chocolate chips, divided**

1 **cup graham cracker crumbs**

1. Prepare and bake cake mix according to package directions for 13×9-inch pan. Cool completely.

2. Microwave marshmallow creme with 1 tablespoon whipping cream in small microwavable bowl on HIGH 30 seconds; stir until smooth. Poke holes in cake at 1-inch intervals with round wooden spoon handle. Pour marshmallow mixture over cake.

3. Combine 1 cup chocolate chips and remaining ¾ cup whipping cream in medium saucepan. Cook and stir over medium heat until chocolate is melted. Remove from heat. Add remaining 1 cup chocolate chips; stir until smooth. Pour melted chocolate over cake. Refrigerate 2 to 3 hours or until firm.

4. Top with graham cracker crumbs just before serving.

Tropical Sugar Cookie Bars

Makes 24 bars

1 package (17½ ounces) sugar cookie mix

⅓ cup canola oil

1 egg

½ cup apricot fruit spread

1 teaspoon grated fresh ginger

1 can (8 ounces) pineapple tidbits, drained

1 fresh mango, peeled, seeded and diced

1 medium kiwi, peeled and diced

2 cups fresh strawberries, stemmed and sliced

1. Preheat oven to 350°F. Line bottom and sides of 13×9-inch baking pan with foil. Coat foil with nonstick cooking spray.

2. Stir cookie mix, oil and egg in medium bowl until well mixed. Spread dough evenly in pan.

3. Bake 23 minutes or until golden. Gently lift cookie out of pan using foil. Cool completely on wire rack.

4. Place fruit spread in small microwavable bowl. Microwave on HIGH 1 minute or until slightly melted. Stir in ginger. Spread apricot mixture evenly over cookie. Arrange fruit over top. Cut into 24 bars.

Watermelon Refresher

Makes 4 servings

6 cups ripe seedless watermelon pieces

¼ cup lemon juice

1 cup chilled champagne

1. Place watermelon in blender; process in two batches until smooth. Strain through sieve into large bowl. Refrigerate until cold.

2. Combine 3 cups watermelon juice and lemon juice in pitcher. Gently stir in champagne. Serve over ice, if desired.

**Tropical
Sugar Cookie Bars**

Individual Fruit Pie

Makes 1 serving

1 refrigerated pie crust (half of a 15-ounce package) or white sandwich bread

2 tablespoons butter

¼ cup cherry, apple or blueberry pie filling

Coarse sugar

1. Cut 1 pie crust into 4 pieces; reserve 2 pieces for another use. Layer 1 tablespoon butter, 1 piece pie crust, cherry pie filling, 1 piece pie crust and 1 tablespoon butter in pie iron. Crimp edge of dough to seal completely.

2. Hold pie iron level over medium coals 6 minutes or until golden brown on each side, turning once. Remove to heatproof surface; carefully remove pie to serving plate. Sprinkle with sugar.

S'more Cones

Makes 4 servings

½ cup mini marshmallows

½ cup chocolate, white chocolate and/or peanut butter chips

Salted peanuts (optional)

4 sugar cones

1. Layer marshmallows, chips and peanuts, if desired, inside of each cone. Place each cone on 6×6-inch piece of foil. Roll up to seal.

2. Place cones around edge of campfire directly on medium coals. Cook 4 minutes or until lightly toasted, turning once. Remove to heatproof surface using large tongs. Cool cones until cool enough to handle.

Crunchy Ice Cream Pie

Makes 6 servings

8 ounces semisweet chocolate, chopped

2 tablespoons butter

1½ cups crisp rice cereal

½ gallon chocolate chip or fudge ripple ice cream, softened

Hot fudge topping

1. Spray 9-inch pie plate with nonstick cooking spray.

2. Combine chocolate and butter in top of double boiler over simmering water; stir until chocolate is melted and mixture is smooth. Remove from heat. Add cereal; stir until well blended.

3. Spoon mixture into prepared pie plate; press onto bottom and 1 inch up side to form crust. Spread ice cream evenly in crust. Cover and freeze until ready to serve.

4. Let pie stand at room temperature 10 minutes before serving. Drizzle with hot fudge topping.

S'more Cones

Mojito

Makes 2 servings

8 **fresh mint leaves, plus additional for garnish**

2 **ounces lime juice**

2 **teaspoons superfine sugar or powdered sugar**

3 **ounces light rum**

Soda water

2 **lime slices (optional)**

Combine 4 mint leaves, lime juice and sugar in each of two highball glasses; mash with wooden spoon or muddler. Fill glass with ice. Pour rum over ice; top with soda water. Garnish with lime slices and remaining mint leaves.

White Sangria

Makes 8 to 10 servings

2 **oranges, cut into ¼-inch slices**

2 **lemons, cut into ¼-inch slices**

½ **cup sugar**

2 **bottles (750 ml each) dry, fruity white wine (such as Pinot Grigio), chilled**

½ **cup peach schnapps**

3 **ripe peaches, pit removed and cut into wedges**

2 **cups ice cubes (about 16 cubes)**

1. Place orange and lemon slices in large punch bowl. Pour sugar over fruit; mash lightly until sugar dissolves and fruit begins to break down.

2. Stir in wine, peach schnapps and peaches; mix well. Refrigerate at least 2 hours or up to 10 hours. Add ice cubes just before serving.

Mojito

Chocolate Chip Skillet Cookie

Makes 8 servings

1¾ cups all-purpose flour

1 teaspoon baking soda

1 teaspoon salt

¾ cup (1½ sticks) butter, softened

¾ cup packed brown sugar

½ cup granulated sugar

2 eggs

1 teaspoon vanilla

1 package (12 ounces) semisweet chocolate chips

Sea salt (optional)

Ice cream (optional)

1. Preheat oven to 350°F or preheat grill grid over campfire.

2. Combine flour, baking soda and 1 teaspoon salt in medium bowl. Beat butter, brown sugar and granulated sugar in large bowl with electric mixer at medium speed until creamy. Beat in eggs and vanilla until well blended. Gradually add flour mixture at low speed; beat just until blended. Stir in chocolate chips. Press batter evenly into well-seasoned* large cast iron skillet. Sprinkle lightly with sea salt, if desired.

3. Bake or cook 35 minutes or until top and edges are golden brown but cookie is still soft in center. Cool on wire rack 10 minutes before cutting into wedges. Serve warm with ice cream, if desired.

*If skillet is not well seasoned, brush lightly with melted butter or vegetable oil.

Easy No-Bake Cocoa Oatmeal Cookies

Makes 2 dozen cookies

1 cup sugar

1 cup flaked coconut

½ cup unsweetened cocoa powder

½ cup creamy peanut butter

½ cup milk

½ teaspoon vanilla

2 cups old-fashioned oats

1. Line cookie sheet with parchment paper.

2. Combine sugar, coconut, cocoa, peanut butter, milk and vanilla in medium saucepan; bring to a boil over medium-high heat. Reduce heat to low; stir in oats until well blended.

3. Drop dough by tablespoonfuls onto prepared cookie sheet. Freeze 1 to 2 hours. Store in refrigerator.

Shirley Temple

Makes 1 serving

8 ounces ginger ale (1 cup)

1 ounce grenadine

Lime wedge, orange slice or maraschino cherry

Fill highball glass half full with ice; top with ginger ale and grenadine. Garnish with lime wedge.

Easy No-Bake Cocoa Oatmeal Cookies

Strawberry Poke Cake

Makes 12 to 15 servings

1 package (about 15 ounces) white cake mix, plus ingredients to prepare mix

2 packages (4-serving size each) strawberry gelatin, plus ingredients to prepare mix

1 container (8 ounces) frozen whipped topping, thawed

1 cup sliced fresh strawberries

1. Prepare and bake cake mix according to package directions for 13×9-inch pan. Cool completely.

2. Prepare gelatin according to package directions for quick set method in two separate medium bowls; chill 15 minutes. Poke holes in cake at ½-inch intervals with round wooden spoon handle. Stir one bowl of gelatin; pour over cake. Reserve remaining bowl. Refrigerate cake 1 hour.

3. Stir remaining gelatin; pour over cake top. Top with whipped topping and strawberries. Refrigerate 2 to 3 hours or until firm.

Sherry Cobbler

Makes 1 serving

½ teaspoon orange liqueur

½ teaspoon simple syrup (recipe follows)

4 ounces dry sherry (amontillado or oloroso)

Orange slice

Fill large wine glass or old fashioned glass three-fourths full with crushed ice; add liqueur and simple syrup. Stir until blended. Gently stir in sherry; garnish with orange slice.

Simple Syrup

Bring 1 cup water to a boil; stir in 1 cup sugar. Reduce heat to low; stir constantly until sugar is dissolved. Cool to room temperature; store syrup in glass jar in refrigerator.

Dad's Ginger Molasses Cookies

Makes about 4 dozen

1 cup shortening

1 cup sugar

1 tablespoon baking soda

2 teaspoons ground ginger

2 teaspoons ground cinnamon

1 teaspoon ground cloves

½ teaspoon salt

1 cup molasses

⅔ cup double-strength instant coffee*

1 egg

4¾ cups all-purpose flour

To prepare double-strength coffee, follow instructions for instant coffee but use twice the recommended amount of instant coffee granules.

1. Preheat oven to 350°F. Lightly grease cookie sheets.

2. Beat shortening and sugar with electric mixer until creamy. Beat in baking soda, ginger, cinnamon, cloves and salt until well blended. Add molasses, coffee and egg, one at a time, beating well after each addition. Gradually add flour, beating on low speed just until blended.

3. Drop dough by rounded tablespoonfuls 2 inches apart onto prepared cookie sheets. Bake 12 to 15 minutes or until cookies are set but not browned. Cool on cookie sheets 1 minute. Remove to wire racks; cool completely.

Fresh Corn Ice Cream

Makes about 6 servings

1 **medium ear corn**

1 **cup whole milk, plus more if necessary**

2 **cups half-and-half**

¼ **cup granulated sugar**

¼ **cup packed light brown sugar**

2 **egg yolks**

¼ **teaspoon vanilla**

¾ **cup chopped salted pecans**

1. Scrape kernels from corn into nonaluminum saucepan. Add corncob. Pour in 1 cup milk. Partially cover and cook over very low heat 30 minutes. (If milk evaporates completely, add ¼ cup more.) Discard corncob.

2. Stir half-and-half, granulated sugar and brown sugar into corn mixture. Cook, uncovered, over low heat, stirring frequently, until sugars dissolve and liquid comes to a simmer.

3. Beat egg yolks in small bowl. Pour about ½ cup corn mixture into egg yolks, stirring constantly. Pour egg yolk mixture into saucepan with corn mixture. Cook over medium heat, stirring, 10 minutes or until slightly thickened. Remove from heat. Stir in vanilla.

4. Pour corn mixture into plastic container, cover and refrigerate until completely cold. (This can be done a day in advance.)

5. Process corn mixture in ice cream machine according to manufacturer's directions. When ice cream is becoming firm, mix in pecans and finish processing.

Peanutty Double Chip Cookies

Makes about 3 dozen

½ cup (1 stick) butter, softened

¾ cup granulated sugar

¾ cup packed brown sugar

2 eggs

1 teaspoon baking soda

1 teaspoon vanilla

2 cups all-purpose flour

1 cup chunky peanut butter

1 cup semisweet or milk chocolate chips

1 cup peanut butter chips

1. Preheat oven to 350°F. Line cookie sheets with parchment paper or spray with nonstick cooking spray.

2. Beat butter, granulated sugar and brown sugar in large bowl with electric mixer at medium speed until blended. Add eggs, baking soda and vanilla; beat until light. Add flour and peanut butter; beat at low speed until dough is stiff and smooth. Stir in chocolate and peanut butter chips. Drop dough by heaping tablespoonfuls 2 inches apart onto prepared cookie sheets. Press down with tines of fork to flatten slightly.

3. Bake 12 minutes or until cookies are set but not browned. *Do not overbake.* Remove to wire racks to cool completely.

Chocolate Cake Stuffed Oranges

Makes 6 servings

6 **large navel oranges**

1 **package (about 18 ounces) chocolate cake mix, plus ingredients to prepare mix**

1. Slice ½ inch off top of stem end of each orange; reserve tops. Hollow out each orange, leaving ½ inch of flesh and peel around bottom and sides. Discard flesh or reserve for another use. Place each orange on 6×6-inch piece of foil sprayed with nonstick cooking spray.

2. Prepare cake mix according to package directions. Fill each orange two-thirds full with cake mix; replace tops of oranges. Roll foil up and around each orange to seal. Place oranges top side up in medium coals around edge of campfire. Cook 1 hour or until toothpick inserted into centers comes out clean. Remove to heatproof surface using large tongs.

Pineapple Rum Agua Fresca

Makes 6 servings

⅓ cup plus ¼ cup sugar, divided

3 cups fresh pineapple chunks (about half of 1 large pineapple)

¼ cup lime juice

2 tablespoons chopped fresh mint

1 cup light rum

1 cup chilled club soda

Fresh mint springs

1. Place ¼ cup sugar in shallow dish. Wet rims of six glasses with damp paper towel; dip rims in sugar.

2. Combine pineapple, remaining ⅓ cup sugar, lime juice and chopped mint in blender; blend 30 seconds to 1 minute or until mixture is frothy.

3. Pour into pitcher; stir in rum and club soda. Serve in prepared glasses over ice. Garnish with mint sprigs.

Index

Acknowledgments

The publisher would like to thank the companies and organizations listed below for the use of their recipes and photographs in this publication.

Campbell Soup Company
Dole Food Company, Inc.
McCormick & Company, Inc.
National Turkey Federation
Pinnacle Foods
Recipes courtesy of the Reynolds Kitchens
Unilever

Metric Conversion Chart

VOLUME MEASUREMENTS (dry)

⅛ teaspoon = 0.5 mL
¼ teaspoon = 1 mL
½ teaspoon = 2 mL
¾ teaspoon = 4 mL
1 teaspoon = 5 mL
1 tablespoon = 15 mL
2 tablespoons = 30 mL
¼ cup = 60 mL
⅓ cup = 75 mL
½ cup = 125 mL
⅔ cup = 150 mL
¾ cup = 175 mL
1 cup = 250 mL
2 cups = 1 pint = 500 mL
3 cups = 750 mL
4 cups = 1 quart = 1 L

VOLUME MEASUREMENTS (fluid)

1 fluid ounce (2 tablespoons) = 30 mL
4 fluid ounces (½ cup) = 125 mL
8 fluid ounces (1 cup) = 250 mL
12 fluid ounces (1½ cups) = 375 mL
16 fluid ounces (2 cups) = 500 mL

WEIGHTS (mass)

½ ounce = 15 g
1 ounce = 30 g
3 ounces = 90 g
4 ounces = 120 g
8 ounces = 225 g
10 ounces = 285 g
12 ounces = 360 g
16 ounces = 1 pound = 450 g

DIMENSIONS

1/16 inch = 2 mm
⅛ inch = 3 mm
¼ inch = 6 mm
½ inch = 1.5 cm
¾ inch = 2 cm
1 inch = 2.5 cm

OVEN TEMPERATURES

250°F = 120°C
275°F = 140°C
300°F = 150°C
325°F = 160°C
350°F = 180°C
375°F = 190°C
400°F = 200°C
425°F = 220°C
450°F = 230°C

BAKING PAN SIZES

Utensil	Size in Inches/Quarts	Metric Volume	Size in Centimeters
Baking or Cake Pan (square or rectangular)	8×8×2	2 L	20×20×5
	9×9×2	2.5 L	23×23×5
	12×8×2	3 L	30×20×5
	13×9×2	3.5 L	33×23×5
Loaf Pan	8×4×3	1.5 L	20×10×7
	9×5×3	2 L	23×13×7
Round Layer Cake Pan	8×1½	1.2 L	20×4
	9×1½	1.5 L	23×4
Pie Plate	8×1¼	750 mL	20×3
	9×1¼	1 L	23×3
Baking Dish or Casserole	1 quart	1 L	—
	1½ quart	1.5 L	—
	2 quart	2 L	—